Woman
Stand Up

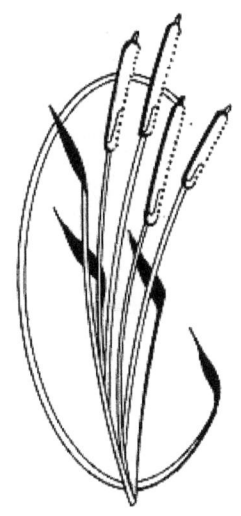

Woman
Stand Up

Nadine V. Hadley

Senior Publisher
Steven Lawrence Hill Sr

ASA Publishing Corporation

A Publisher Trademark Title page

ASA Publishing Corporation
An Accredited Publishing House with the BBB
www.asapublishingcorporation.com

The Landmark Building
23 E. Front St., Suite 103, Monroe, Michigan 48161

All Rights Reserved. No part of this publication may be reproduced, stored in a retrieval system or transmitted in any form or by any means electronic, mechanical, photocopying, recording or otherwise, without the prior written permission of the publisher. Author/writer rights to "Freedom of Speech" protected by and with the "1st Amendment" of the Constitution of the United States of America. This is a work of non-fiction; religious freedom of prayer and worship. Any resemblance to actual events, locales, person living or deceased that is not related to the author's literacy is entirely coincidental.

With this title/copyrights page, the reader is notified that the publisher does not assume, and expressly disclaims any obligation to the authors own workings, within the author's rights as manuscript owner. Nor is the publisher obligated to obtain and/or include any other information other than that provided by the author (unless permitted) and within the ownership rights thereof. Any belief system, promotional motivations, including but not limited to the use of non-fictional/fictional characters and/or characteristics of this book, are within the boundaries of the author's own creativity in order to reflect the nature and concept of the book.

Any and all vending sales and distribution not permitted without full book cover and this copyright page.

Copyrights
©2018 Nadine V. Hadley, All Rights Reserved
Book Title: Woman Stand Up
Date Published: 10.08.2018 / Edition 1 *Trade Paperback*
Book ID: ASAPCID2380766
ISBN: 978-1-946746-40-5
Library of Congress Cataloging-in-Publication Data

This book was published in the United States of America
Great State of Michigan

A Publisher Trademark Copyrights page

Table of Contents

Introduction ....(a)

I'm a Winter Woman 1

Career Woman 5

Kingdom Woman 9

The Women of Divorce 13

Single Parent Woman 17

Sermon: Mother Hang in There! 21

A MOTHER'S PRAYER 25

A Widow Woman 29

Woman of Achievement 33

Married Woman 35

Single Woman 39

Conclusion of the Whole Matter 43

Introduction

Woman yes you can . . .

Do all things through Christ that strength you.

Woman yes you can . . .

Be the head and not the tail, above only and not beneath.

Yes, I did not know who you were talking about, but NOW I know I'm ready to give Jesus PRAISE because he brought me out a miry clay. I did not come to look cute. I came to this church because he brought me out of darkness and into his light. I didn't come to see you, you, or even you. I came to lift up the name of Jesus who loved me when I was out of control, and used bad language. You know them 4 letter words. Oh, you know what I'm talking about! You have not been saved all your life! Yes, my dress is tight and short. But I needed God so like yesterday I had no time to check out what I was wearing. And yes, my cleavage is showing and what up!! Somebody said to come as you are. I'm here now - what about this eternal life you all are talking about, that's what I heard the church people say. I want some of that!!!

Nope, my children aren't in church but they got a chance too now. They see their mother has change. I got to give God the Glory due Him and the Honor. He's worthy, I owe Him my life. I'm Grateful, Humble, Committed, Faithful and Thankful to even be welcomed in Jesus's family. I can't live no longer without Him. This new man is the lover of my Soul!!!! I put that SUGAR DADDY down. He is no match for who I got NOW!

Now I'm a Tither. Now I'm helping others that was just like I use to be. Now I'm giving out the little bit that I got in finances, and that keeps on multiplying.

I can not beat God giving. Jesus . . . God in the flesh. That's what the Bible told me.

Now I study to show myself approved. Walking up right to do those things pleasing in my Lord's sight. I even got longer dresses and cover up my lady body parts. Also wearing shoes to dance my way in heaven. I tell everybody about Jesus. Old things are passed away, all things become new. My kids are even going to church.

Do you like the new Me? God does and that's good enough for me." Amen, Amen!!

Woman
Stand Up

Nadine V. Hadley

I'm a Winter Woman

Stand UP Woman . . .

1 Timothy 5:2 NKJV

older women as mothers, younger women as sisters with all purity.

Titus 2:3-5 NKJV

3) *the older women likewise, that they be reverent in behavior, not slanderers, not given to much wine, teachers of good things-*
4) *that they admonish the young women to love their husbands, to love their children,*
5) *to be discreet, chaste, homemakers, good, obedient to their own husbands, that the word of God may not be blasphemed.*

Yes, I'm a Single Woman and waiting on the Lord. He has shown me how to do the right thing in marriage this time. Yes I made some mistakes, but I learned along the way what to do and what not to do. First of all, I didn't know what the bible says about marriage. I was not saved . . . young, . . . self-centered and it was all about me, me, me! I've learned to put God first in everything. He's concern about your Soul and motives. Prayer Changes Things. Read the Word of the God the first part of your day. And pray a personal prayer and wait for the Holy

Spirit to give you instruction for the day. It takes God to order our step.

    First ladies be an example of the women coming behind you. Holiness, Humble, a Women of Honor. That is much needed today when new believers join a church. A warm hug and a welcome back for the next service. As a Season Woman we got to win souls for Christ. Make disciples everywhere you go! The World is looking for the love we have for one another. Love goes a long way. Love covers protects, shields!

    Stay faithful to God. Keep a forgiving heart not holding faults against another. None of us are perfect! We all need Jesus. Amen, amen!!!!!!!!!

Career Woman

Woman Stand Up . . .

Acts 9:36 NKJV

36) *At Joppa there was a certain disciple named Tabitha, which is translated Dorcas. This woman was full of good works and charitable deeds which*

she did.

There are some of us women don't mine working and sometimes even getting our hands dirty. We are Firefighters at home and on the job. We are labor workers, construction workers CEO, principal teachers at schools and colleges. Bus drivers, waitresses, you name it we got our hands in it. And who would have ever thought we would have a woman running for President of the United States.

The platform has been wide open for us. We can do all things for Christ that strengthen us. We as women are making a difference in walking with authority in Christ. We are being kept by Jesus makes us have these opportunities to walk in these open doors. *Ask* and it shall be given, *Seek* and you shall fine, *Knock* and the door will be open unto you. May God get the Glory!!!

We also don't have the back seat in Voting!

Stand Up Woman we are on the move to make things better. Still, letting if married our husband be the Priest of the Home. Still be Submitted as a Wife. Give Honor where Honor is due. Amen!!

Kingdom Woman

Women Stand Up . . .

Judges 4:4

Now Deborah, a prophetess, the wife of Lapidoth was judging Israel at that time.

There are some Women are Apostles, Bishop, Pastors, running full Ministries. And having some with husbands backing them and not minding their wives in clergy position. That's God!!

When Mary was with Child of the Holy Spirit, Joseph had to step back and not touch his wife until after Jesus was born. The Lord will never lead you to do wrong. Trust him lean not to your own understanding. In all your ways acknowledge him and he shall direct your path.

Kingdom work is not as easiest as just preaching. Your life style has to match up with your position. Holy Living in every area of your personality. Kind, Humble, Management of home and business well. Love working with people for kingdom in reaching Souls. Staying in the Prayer room with open communication with God. Pure Heart, a Worshiper, a Woman that Praise God in the storm. Upholding chastity if not married. Devoted and Faithful to the

Ministry of office you hold. So Woman Stand Up!!!!!

A Kingdom Woman can chase out devils and plead the Blood of Jesus! Lay hand on the sick and they shall recover! Go in the enemy's camp and take back what he stole, your joy, your peace of mind!

Do it for God to get the Glory! Dedicated yourself to the Lord not for to be famous or seen. But let people see the Christ in you. It's all about Jesus anyhow. Amen!

The Woman of Divorce

Women Stand Up . . .

John 4:17 NKJV

17) *The women answered and said, "I have no husband."*
Jesus said to her, "You have well said, 'I have no

husband,'..."

Yes, divorce is one of the most hurting things you could ever be tested with. But guess what, Girl friend? You're still standing! God can still use you for great things. Number 1 you know what to tell one what traps the Devil fights you in marriage and how you fight in prayer. You'll learn He that find a wife find a good thing and obtain favor with the Lord. And the Lord can keep you if you wanted to be kept.

Take time to get to know your Maker. Fine out what makes you happy. Learn the new you! You are special to God after all he made you in his image. Find out in your prayers to the Master your goals and destiny he had before the foundation of the world.

Woman Stand UP God's still writing chapters about you. When you have given your all and done your best. What more could be done. You gave and forgive. Now forgive yourself!!!!

Make a promise to God no sex before

marriage. Let's just do it God's way. He knows what best for you. Tell the Lord in detail what you want and let that man find you as a wife he wants to love for the rest of his life. This time make sure you both have the same mind set about God. How can two walk together unless they agree. It will happen for the best of us. Amen!

Single Parent Woman

Stand Up Woman . . .

Ephesians 6:2

2) *"Honour thy father and mother," which is the first commandment with promise:*

Yes you can . . .

Do all things through Christ that strengthen you!

Our role as a single mother has came to not only buy the bacon, but fry the bacon. Can I get a witness!

Helping in doing homework with the kids after a 8 hour shift job. Washing clothes at night when you should be sleeping. Setting up rules and chores. Family dinners and talking about their day by keeping the communication open. No late night TV on school night. No, they can't always have the latest shoes or style shirts. But they're clean with bathes, and hair combed. Boys hair cut, washes behind their ears. Face wash, teeth brushed, deodorant on, and well-mannered children.

Who said a single mother can't have a Doctor or a Lawyer come out of her household. Prayer and fasting dedicated to God. There is nothing to hard for God!! Wait, Pray, and depend on Jesus. Hold fast and don't let go of his hand. Walk by faith and not by sight. Amen, amen!

Sermon:

Mother Hang in There!

I'm a praying Mother. Prayer has changed so many solutions from home to job for my family, the list goes on and on.

Psalm 22:10 NKJV

10) *I was cast upon You from birth. From My mother's womb You have been My God.*

Psalm 27:10 NKJV

10) *When my father and my mother forsake me, Then the LORD will take care of me.*

Psalm 102;13 NKJV

13) *You will arise and have mercy on Zion; For the time to favor her; Yes, the set time, has come.*

    We serve a right now God. He will never leave us or forsake us. Our faith got to believe he will do whatever we ask in his Word in the name of Jesus. Eyes have not seen ears have not heard nor has it entered in the heart of (man or woman) what God has prepared for us.

Job 22:28 NKJV

28) *You will also declare a thing a thing, And it will*

be established for you; So light will shine on your ways.

Psalm 113:9 NKJV

9) *He grants the barren woman a home, Like a joyful mother of children.*

Praise the Lord! My favor mother story is Hannah, Samuel's mother. It's in 1 Samuel Chapter 1:1-28. READ THAT STORY IT WILL BLESS A MOTHER'S LIFE. If you love the Word of God like I do the bible is your favor Book!

"Mother Hang in There"

Matthew 19:19 NKJV

19) *"Honor your father and your mother, and, 'You shall love your neighbor as yourself."*

When Jesus did his first miracle his mother knew what was in him at the wedding.

John2:5 NKJV

5) *His mother said to the servants, "Whatever He says to you, do it."*

    When a mother carry a child for nine month they become bond to each other. He or She pick up feelings good and bad even in the womb. We got to be careful what we put in our body food and all!

    Stay Praying for your children and train them up in the fear of the Lord. Mother hang in there! Children will be taught of the Lord and great is their peace! Amen!!

A MOTHER'S PRAYER

Father God in the name of Jesus I have train up my children in your way they should go. And to have respect for your Holy Word. I want them to walk in your truth and integrity that they may have favor with God and man. None of us are perfect but I want them to strive for it. Let me be the type of

Mother that they could trust to be open to talk about in what's going on in life problems or good times. Teach them to Honor and be Faithful in Church. Incline their ear to your Word. A humble and submissive prayer life. Compassionate to their Pastor and obey those that have rule over them. And always putting God first in every area of their lives. And please Jesus to know you are God and no one comes to the Father except by you. And that's in your name every knee shall bow, and every tongue shall confess that Jesus is Lord. PLUS, a strong relationship with you! Hallelujah, Amen!!!!

And to honor their father and their mother so their days may be long on the earth. I plead the Blood over their lives. Satan the Lord rebuke you! You can't have their soul, mind, peace, or joy! They are covered by the Blood of Jesus that was shed on Calvary. Let them love and respect authority and give honor where honor is due. Let no sick or disease cleave to their bodies. Let no weapon formed against them prosper. I pray over to watch the company they keep, be godly children. And check their internet connections. Only you know Lord! Get the Glory and the Praise out of their lives Jesus, Amen, amen!!

A Widow Woman

Woman Stand Up!

1 Timothy 5:3 NKJV

3) *Honour widows that are widows indeed.*

As a Widow Woman it's not easy to deal with life especially if you had no children. You miss your

Husband so bad it's been hard to cope with life to go on. You have your good days and bad. You wonder is there anybody that could love you in a way that's needed now. And if you're in Ministries, can that next person handle your anointing that is on your life, and stand in the gap and pray you through? Can he catch in the spirit like an eagle?!!!!!

We as women have been in a fight with the devil since Eve. But Sister Girl We Have Already Won!!!! The battle is not yours, it's the Lords. Hang on, God's got your tears and it's not wasted. He's in touch with your feelings. Loneliness, Depression, sad sometimes even angry that his life was shorten right when you were glad to be in his arms. Lord why did he have to die so young? Death have its way of taking its toll on you, kind of leave you limp. Lord I'm still young enough to enjoy my womanhood and maybe even have a child. You say Lord He that findeth a wife finds a good thing and obtain Favor with The Lord. I'm waiting on you Jesus!!!! Hold and kept me until he comes. It gets hard on me Lord. I know you understand. But I know it's in your hand and you're in control. You did it once I know you can do it again. I Love you Lord through it all, I trust you even in this. Show up and show out I pray. Amen!!

And widows that have children that are grown is a blessing. They can all pitch in and help their mother in this time of grieving with this whole family lost. God got a way of working things out, so you can cope and be comfort by Love ones and friends. We have such an understanding Father in heaven. He knows what suffering is about. He sent his Son to experience every heart-ache we would ever have it go through. That's why he says 2 Corinthians 4:11 "For we which live are always delivered unto death for Jesus sake, that the life also of Jesus might be made manifest in our mortal flesh." So that lets us know we will see our love ones again. Amen!!!

Woman of Achievement

Woman Stand Up . . .

1 Corinthians 9:27 NKJV

27) *But I discipline my body and bring it into subjection, lest when I have preached to others, I myself should become disqualified.*

Yes We can . . .

There are Godly Women in the athletic arena that have won Gold Medals. In Tennis, Swimming, Track, Basketball, they have humbled themselves with their training to be the best in the county. Some have also went on to the Olympics and Won Trophies!!!

We also have achieved in Music, became Actors, Models, Photographers, News Directors, Architects and the list goes on and on.

Ladies What You Want To Do in theses last days for your God!!!!!! The blessing of the Lord, it maketh rich, he addeth no sorrow with it. We as women have climb Jacob's ladder. There is no stopping us now!! Let my light shine so men can see my good works and Glorify my Father in Heaven. Amen!

Married Woman

Ephesians 5:22 NKJV

22) *Wives submit to your own husband, as to the Lord.*

You are now Mrs., no longer Miss. And marriage is honorable, and the bed is undefiled. God hates divorces, so he would love for you to stay together until death do you part. Respect your husband and submit to his authority as Priest of the household. Your body now belongs to your husband and vice versa. The only time you are to deprive each other from making love is in during fasting and prayer. But come together again so Satan don't tempt you in lack of self-control.

It is best to marry someone of your same religion beliefs. Male and Female is what God honors.

Marriage is a three-fold cord not easily broken. Put God first in your lives. Touch and agree in prayer on often like daily. For a successful relationship tell the truth in love and don't go to bed angry. Talk things out in a humble and loving way. Have no problem to say I'm sorry and forgive me. You also be forgiving. Nobody is perfect. Support each other in compliments. Little gifts and cards keep the fire burning in each other hearts. Still look and dress sexy even at home!! Have date night!! Watch sports with him if that's what he like. Candlelight dinner in fixing his favor meal. Clean house and tell him you love him everyday. And, find a church home to fellowship. Amen!

Single Woman

Yes you are . . .

Philippians 4:3NKJV

3) *And I urge you also, true companion, help these women who labored with me in the gospel, with Clement also and the rest of my fellow workers,*

whose names are in the Book of Life.

Miss Lady, you are holding up a holy standard for the Lord. Life is freely open for your enjoyment. Worship the Lord in spirit and in truth. Devote your life to Prayer and Fasting. The Father don't mine you working, going to school, traveling and seeing this wonderful world He's made. He gives us all things to enjoy that life more abundantly.

Ask the Lord to keep you close to him until he send your Soul-Mate. But in the meantime, learn yourself and find out what makes you happy. The joy of the Lord is your strength. Have set time for prayer every morning and every night. You're His girl and He loves you and will never leave you, nor forsake you. Communicate with the Father about details of your plans in relationship, work, and leisure. I shall live and not die and declare the works of the Lord. Amen!

So Woman of God, Bless you are when The

Creator of all Things is your Savior. Peace be with you forever!!! And love the Lord's House of Prayer! Amen, amen!!!!!

Conclusion of the Whole Matter

God has always loved us from the start. He pulled us out of Man so it will be no mistake we are bone of his bone and flesh of his flesh. Of course we suppose to make it happen with the help of God. Thank God for Jesus, he wanted us to have life and have life more abundantly. The Good Life!

We were the first ones at the tomb when our Savior died early on Sunday morning to anoint his body. He has been always on our mind once he saved us. We are sensitive to his ways. God called us both Adam. No we don't have seeds, but we carry the seed.

So what have God birth in you Woman of God? Carry it full term then, let it work for you. Write the vision, make it plain. God is not a man, that He should lie. Neither the son of man, that He should repent: hath He said, and shall He not do it? Or hath He spoken, and shall He not make it good?

Soar in these last days! Your destiny is complete in our Lord of lords and King of kings!

It's getting late in the evening and the sun is going down. Do it Girl Friend! Woman, Yes You Can!!

WOMAN STAND UP!!!!

Amen!

www.ingramcontent.com/pod-product-compliance
Lightning Source LLC
Chambersburg PA
CBHW061513040426
42450CB00008B/1605